CALIFORNIA STATE UNIVERSITY, SACRAMENTO

This book is due on the last date stamped below.
Failure to return books on the date due will result in assessment
of overdue fees.

Also available in the series:

Eve Names the Animals by Susan Donnelly
Rain by William Carpenter

The Morse Poetry Prize
Edited by Guy Rotella

SUE ELLEN THOMPSON

This Body of Silk

THE 1986 MORSE
POETRY PRIZE
SELECTED AND
INTRODUCED BY
X. J. KENNEDY

Northeastern University Press
BOSTON

Designer: Ann Twombly

Northeastern University Press
Copyright © 1986 by Sue Ellen Thompson

Library of Congress Cataloging in Publication Data

Thompson, Sue Ellen, 1948–
  This body of silk.

  (Morse Poetry Prize : 1986)
  I. Kennedy, X. J. II. Title. III. Series
PS3570.H6438T5 1986   811'.54   86–12465
ISBN 0–930350–96–0 (pbk. : alk. paper)

Composed in Weiss by Eastern Typesetting Company,
South Windsor, Connecticut. Printed and bound at the
Alpine Press, Stoughton, Massachusetts. The paper is
Warren's No. 66 Antique, an acid-free sheet.

MANUFACTURED IN THE UNITED STATES OF AMERICA
91 90 89 88 87 86   5 4 3 2 1

for Frank A. Williams, Jr.

> ". . . while I
> Saw morning harden upon the wall,
> Unmoved, unknowing
> That your great going
> Had place that moment, and altered all."
> —Thomas Hardy, "The Going"

ACKNOWLEDGMENTS

The poems in this volume have appeared in the following magazines: *Chiaroscuro* ("Son et Lumière," "Wholesale Hardware, Retired"); *The Connecticut Writer* ("The Newlyweds," "The Swing"); *Croton Review* ("Equinox," "Meantime, Greenwich"); *Denver Quarterly* ("The Compliment," "Indian Summer"); *Footwork* ("The Surprise Party," "A Mother to Her Daughter"); *A Letter Among Friends* ("The Snow, Among Other Things"); *New Letters* ("The Death of Uncles"); *Poet Lore* ("Cold Comfort"); *Poetry Now* ("To a Friend, Upon Opening His Offices for Complete Financial Management"); *Poets On* ("Knees," "The Swimming Lesson"); *Red Fox Review* ("Nude at the Ironing Board"); *Tendril* ("Family Portrait").

Contents

Thaw *xv*

I. THE SHADOW OF HOME

Son et Lumière *3*
Equinox *5*
Wholesale Hardware, Retired *6*
Moths *8*
The Surprise Party *10*
Falling Awake *11*

II. LOOKING FOR WHAT WE KNOW

Cold Comfort *15*
Pen Pals *16*
Family Portrait *17*
To a Friend, Upon Opening His Offices
    for Complete Financial Management *19*
Insomniac *20*
Biology *22*
Breakfast in Key West *24*

III. THE WHOLE OF LONGING

Today a Wedding *29*
Nude at the Ironing Board *30*
The Snow, Among Other Things *31*
Mean Time, Greenwich *32*
The Compliment *33*

The Newlyweds 34

Flying Over Connecticut 36

Photograph of a Storm at Watch Hill 38

Midsummer 39

August 40

September 41

Indian Summer 42

Excuses 43

IV   IN THIS A CELEBRATION

Underwater 47

Postpartum 49

The Swimming Lesson 51

Conversation in Key West 53

Hypothermia 54

The Swing 55

Love Letters 57

Girl of Four 58

A Father to His Daughter 59

A Mother to Her Daughter 61

Biceps 63

V   THIS BODY OF SILK

Birthdays 67

Knees 68

When You Go to the Funeral 70

The Sinking of the *Marques* 72

Letter to Diane 74

The Death of Uncles 76

Unk at Eighty-four 77

An Old Man Falls 78

Introduction

Tradition decrees that the writer of an introduction to a prize-winning book of poems justify, as best he can, having chosen it for print in the first place. In an effort to convince readers of the wisdom of his choice, he is tempted to praise the winner in desperate superlatives.

Fortunately, Sue Ellen Thompson's rich, precise poems need no trumpets sounded before them. Their quality will naturally show itself. I admired them on first look, though I have to confess to feeling, at the start, a few reservations. As a sometime foreman of poetry workshops, I have read far too many lyrics by autoerotic undergraduates praising their own lustrous hair and the "sleek admirability" of their own flesh (I quote from memory); and when first I spied the title *This Body of Silk*, I muttered, oh-oh, another one.

Luckily, this fear proved groundless. As that unique poem "Birthdays" reveals, the speaker's body is no static object of adoration, but the body of a toiling, perspiring runner. And the phrase "body of silk" refers as well to a hot-air balloon in the sky, its delicate form like the runner's feet rising and falling. Other metaphors impinge. As in dream, the runner's strides take her back to her earlier years: to running away from a boy who had chased her in grammar school, to running lest she be late for her wedding. I can only begin to sketch the complexity of this wonderful, synechdochic poem.

Another doubt I had, which went away more slowly, is a doubt I feel toward much new poetry in a time when most poets have thrown over belief in the hoary verities of rhyme and meter. Thompson does not adhere to such a traditional faith, except in "Unk at Eighty-four," in which an old man addresses us in rhyme (perhaps to suggest his decrepit antiquity). In other poems, she seems half in love with half-rhyme; and much of the time she writes in a kind of liberal meter. If in her work the ghost of traditional form lurks behind the arras, as T. S. Eliot said it lurks in all interesting free verse, usually she lets it moan there unobtrusively. I guessed that, were many of these poems not to be divided into lines but to be set as prose poems in solid blocks, surprisingly little harm would be done to them. But I don't feel this doubt in reading Thompson's every poem, not in the last lines of "Flying Over Connecticut," a memoir of receiving an unexpected, surreptitious kiss ("so shadowy and swift / it might have been the passing / of a plane"):

> But I tell you now, for weeks
> I held that kiss like the fixed
> pattern of frost on a window, surprised
> by its delicate two-dimensionality,
> always looking through, beyond.

The lines seem right and inevitable, and where they break on the words *fixed* and *surprised*, the fractures crackle with energy.

In the end, I became aware that, God forbid, I shouldn't expect Thompson to worship in my own temple. And I found her poetry affording me deep pleasures other than those of strict meter and rhyme and inevitable line-endings. At all times, Thompson works like a skilled surgeon, with tremendous assurance, and it is a joy to watch her operate. Hers is an alert and playful spirit, generous yet discriminating, warmly involved with those close to her. At most times, her angle of vision seems obviously that of a woman, and the experiences are those only a woman may know: birth, maternity, finding mother-and-daughter affinities. But Thompson understands the other sex deeply. Witness "Unk at Eighty-four," or "A Father to His Daughter," in which a man recalls (for the girl's illumination) his once confronting that strange creature, a female, and feeling himself awkwardly, painfully young.

These poems abound in such wry experiences. Often they surprise with an abrupt table-turning—as in the witty "Family Portrait," whose subject is not (as we initially expect) the male teacher accused of cradle-robbing, but—if I read it right—our need for self-congratulatory indignation. Full of such sharp-eyed perceptions, the poems are intently alive, too, in their figures of speech. Women lifting weights make "slow parentheses in air." The poet recalls her mother's production of ironed shirts:

> They'd hang like tired children
> from the doorknobs, waiting to be sent
> to their rooms.

To the open forms she favors, Thompson brings a musician's astute ear. She speaks of a rich man "awash in the sun's hard cash," of a baby's "milk-drunk smile." Here is a poetry of intelligence and compassion, in evenly balanced quantities.

X. J. KENNEDY

⚡ Thaw

We dress foolishly in light sweaters,
work savagely in the yard, clearing
the way for certain death. Our hearts
are buoyant with promises to ourselves
and to each other: There will be no more
drifts piled in silence against the door,
no more ice-hardened branches
tapping at our sleep. Like buds
we bare ourselves thoughtlessly to this
season's brief flirtation, believing
as always that this time it's love.

And for the time it is enough. To believe
in our own foolishness is enough,
is what passes for Spring in this state
of rock-studded stick-to-itiveness
where any pale show of light
is enough to send us careening
off on bicycles we've practically forgotten
how to ride, off to the shore
to fill our pockets with stones.

PART I

The Shadow of Home

ᔔ *Son et Lumière*

Dusk descends like a tapestry, draping
the walls in armorial reds and golds.
From my perch in the backyard swing set
I hear the day's history rise
pre-recorded from a shrubbery moat:
the summoning of housepets; bath water
ringing down the pipes;
a child's protests, distant
and foreign; the noisy pageantry
of meals. Light takes aim
from an upstairs window, glances
off a banister where socks hang
in formation. More lights, a banner
of lit windows bringing shape
to the shadow of home. A passing car
illuminates the silent massing of white
clapboards, shutters heralding a well-
timed gust. Music swells
from the ground floor, where costumed figures
in robes the color of torchlight move
from room to room in rehearsed slow
motion and strangely modern slippers.

Tonight I am a tourist in the country
of great white houses, resting
on this swing that, swaying,
rocks history into dreams. That I
will take any of this with me
when I fold my map tomorrow
at breakfast seems unlikely.
But I am taken in by this local
spectacle, how simply they live
amid such a splendor of comforts:

the *tching* of silver and glass, the small
light drawing darkness up
the stairs, the blue shawl of trees
pulled tight around the sleeping house.

ᴥ Equinox

(for my father)

I'm breaking a trail for both of us
and thinking of men who drop dead
at sixty-two with little or no
exertion. I hear your breath at my heels
and wonder if it came down to that
would I give you mouth-to-mouth
(and whisper to your lungs, "They taught me that
in college!")? Saved, I'd bear you back
on a litter made of willow switch
and vow to leave poetry behind,
study word processing. We're skiing
on the edge of Spring—a thought that strikes
me now as strangely as that you're my father,
and our skis strike a frozen field
that will be a river before we're done.

Wholesale Hardware, Retired

A pressed tin sky, the back room
a cityscape of boxes, their yellow labels
the bare glow of windows in winter.
The only real window is painted
green. Forty-one years
submerged in this light, sorting
screws and weighing wooden knobs,
the floor soft with spilled
coffee and curls of tape.

It was world enough when he was young,
careless with pin-ups and a toilet
only regulars were bold enough
to use. Now time's high water
marks line the walls: A skinny Girl
Scout, thick braids anchoring
her head to a chest blooming
with merit badges, certification
for a life spent swimming, star-
gazing, naming flowers. A bride
celestial in tea-colored lace,
curls in perfect orbit around
a face planetary under spotlights.
A baby's milk-drunk smile against
her mother's milk-stained dress.

The day he went into hock to buy
this place from the sonofabitch
who almost fired him
once, whose name still rides in gold
above the green glass tide, flashes
its gills like the brass on a sampleboard
at sunset. Whatever it was he wanted

bad enough then to borrow for
he must have had and lost
or he'd be missing it now.

⚓ Moths

There have been doors
I would not open
because of them. And nights
where sleep was broken
by their seasonal tattoo.
From my knotty pine walled
bedroom, circa 1962,
I saw the porchlight muffled
by the dust that sifted
from their wings. That night
I dreamed they lifted
me, Lilliputian-style,
down to Lake Champlain,
where I was forced to kneel
before the walleyed pike
who'd made me drop
my father's rod and reel.
Rooted to this choice
of death by wing or water,
I called out to the only god
I knew, and took
my chances as a daughter.

Ten years later,
we approached the light that marked
the evening's end. Inside,
I knew my father
cursed your skin, as dark
and humid as the rainy night
that suddenly closed in
upon us. On the screen,
a pale green luna

twitched but would not move.
You took my hand
inside your own to prove
that he was harmless, pressed
my finger lightly down
upon his patterned back.
I knew then I lacked
the courage to become your wife,
that if I had to choose
my death by wing or water,
I'd ask forgiveness from the only
god I knew, and take
my chances as a daughter.

The Surprise Party

Last night we argued motherhood. You said
what you always say, that each of us
was wanted and that desire struck like a bell,
clearly and at perfect intervals. For ten years
your milk ran blue, and when Daddy
took you out for dinner you spoiled
your dress with missing us.

I talked about the labor room, the endless light
and furious regret, the long nights
pummeled into sleeplessness by two
small fists as firm and red as vegetables.
It was a time when infants rolled
out car doors, sprouted wings, and cruised
the countryside, open-mouthed, while we
who were mistaken drove on in heavenly neglect.

Tangled with my siblings in this dark closet
as if in one womb, I hear hollow
footsteps cross the porch, the smack of kisses
and hellos muffled by more than distance. Now
we develop houses, husbands, small appendages
of our own and the first gray hairs. It's
your birthday and there are five of us—
all healthy—waiting to be born.

❧ Falling Awake

Swimming somewhere near
sleep but not in
it, as restless
as the wind that lifts
itself, greasy and pale,
from the shallow bed
of the Gulf at dawn, I
see a man leaning
over a woman bending
to lift a banded tulip
from the shallow waters
off Sanibel—his
shoulders shading her
shoulders from the prickly
sun of late April, their
elbows discussing the shell's
muscled turns in its shades
of flesh. Their bodies cup
the sea, faces merged
in wonder at its
single, perfect fruit.

How simple their shape
against the green, against
a sky white at noon
with the steady light
of an egg. How simple
to love one man for forty
years, feet rooted in the same
swift tide that carries
them now before me
as I struggle for sleep
on a night abandoned by all

the wrong men, loose
in the skin they have tried
to take from me, bruised
by the light of this slow
dawn. How simple
it once was to fall
asleep. Or so
it seems, falling
awake to this dream
of my parents on their
anniversary, bending to lift
a tulip, a shell—empty
now of all but the light
of spring and of the flesh.

PART II

Looking
for
What
We
Know

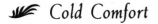 ## Cold Comfort

(for Bird)

Friendship (or whatever ship it is that bobs
at anchor between two women on such distant shores)
lies strangely still tonight. The moon is pale
and wearing thin beyond the glass that robs
us of its waning. The lamp is on. The doors
are shut. But something in us fails

to catch the lines we toss across the room
to save a sinking need. We share
a house tonight as we did that year
in Vermont, a farmhouse strewn
with winter's casual debris. Your hair
reminds me of the dawn you stood in fear

above me, white gathering in your eyes, a crust
of white sifting from your shoulders, white
in your sleeping hair. "The heat's gone off," you said.
I sat up stiff, and snow fell like dust
in my lap. Sitting here with you tonight
conclusion of that fear takes shape: instead

of being wrapped in summer's conscious flesh
we might have slept through middle age. The skin
of our thighs luffs gently as we rearrange
our legs for sleep. I see your belly stretched
about the child soon to join the men
already grown between us. We can change

none of it, nor can we summon up the snow
that slept with us that night. And yet I miss
the simple fact of life that bound us there
in dawn's cold comfort. I go
to bed thinking of what is frayed between us:
The dust that fills my lap, the snow that clings to your hair.

🖋 Pen Pals

(for Anne LeGoff)

As teenagers we dreamed of chilly summers
in London, browsing for books or nibbling
strawberries on some slippery bank;
of noisy American autumns, watching
the cheerleaders' knees turn rosy
in the tattered light. You sent
me strong black tea my parents
wouldn't let me drink, clotted
cream from Devonshire that never looked
quite right for eating. I can't
remember when it was I knew
we'd never meet. A month or two
let slip, then silence

Broken now after twenty years, three
husbands, five children and one more body
of water between us. I had to read
your letter twice to find out
who you are, with your French
man's name, an address where vowels
grow wild. You say you are the postmistress
for your village, that a letter from the States
came through last week; you touched it
and the past wheeled overhead, swift
and clear as the Channel birds over Brittany.

Anne, I can't say what it is
to live in America. Jean-Luc, Yvette,
Laurent, Solange may as well be the names
of stars. But I write to say
that we still have our work before us:
looking for what we know,
to see that it gets where it's going.

✍ Family Portrait

(for Booker)

I agree it looks bad on the surface:
mature man (a teacher), seventeen-year-old
girl (daughter's best friend), his wife
of twenty-three years devoted
(absolutely devoted) to him; his school
up in arms, her school up
in arms, the two of them conspiring
to ruin the unprincipled bastard,
the goddamned cradle-snatcher.

What could be worse? A man,
his daughter, the family dog? The mind
that cannot support such imaginings must
look elsewhere for indignation, must start
somewhere: the cat cruising the myrtled banks,
plundering our righteous refuse on garbage night,
leaving his scent on a discarded
sofa, listening under the porch
for the sound of a family breaking up;

The dog wearing a jacket that cost twice
what it cost her owner to have her spayed,
the trash containing perfectly good sweaters
with strained elbows, a silver spoon mangled
by the dispose-all, moles with punctured spines,
birds with broken necks, poisoned pets,
unborn babies unconceived, inconceivable waste
in the form of hair brushings, paper crumplings,
arguments over nothing, the last word, siblings

Cast aside—Look! Someone has thrown
out a photograph, a perfectly good family

portrait: a man, his devoted wife, their daughter,
the family dog fixed in indignation forever
on the good sofa with the velvet arms, dressed
to kill, hair brushed, the dog looking
so well fed, the father's elbow
crooked protectively around the girl's neck,
the wife with her spine so straight.

To a Friend, Upon Opening His Offices for Complete Financial Management

(for Jimmy)

You painted your kitchen window sills
persimmon, wore your long red
hair behind you like a sunset.
You said a musician has only two
themes: being in love or on the road.
That was the year I drove you to work
while you planned your West Coast Tour,
let you drum on the Pontiac's swollen seats.
Remember the night before
you left for Los Angeles? Humming
along to a rhythmless snow we missed
our exit and sang off the road.
There, on the Pontiac's chilled vinyl
couch, we wrestled and pinned
by moolight said our good-byes.
Later, you wrote me a song:
"Susie, I need a haircut,"
it went. O James
it breaks my heart to hear
of your success, to see your life
engraved on good white stock,
to imagine the view from the penthouse
suite (West Alameda,
opposite Catalina Street),
to "R.S.V.P. by phone, Lorraine."

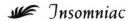 *Insomniac*

(for Richard)

Here is a man who knows his stars,
who feels their gaze familiar as pin-
pricks of sun piercing the green crochet
of spring. His canopy is held aloft by spars
of light; below, the full moon spins
its mountain tops until their motion fades
to tarnished silver. If it spills
its milky light across the floor,
he tells no one, but clement on his hands
and knees forgives the nightly accident, refills
the moon's bright cup. If we could afford
these hours, surely we would spend
them furbishing our French or reading,
always reading. He shrugs, as if to say
we fool ourselves imagining the darkness changes
anything, that his accomplishments are fleeting
as our own. Take this house, the way
its Northern stillness rearranges
the priorities of sound: the wooden floors
shift in their sleep, the refrigerator coughs
to life, and when it rains the flue
grieves on the hearth. The animals slam doors
in their search for food, the stars rush off
to school, shivering in their pale blue
windbreakers. We awake to find
that our boots have been cleaned, our skis bound
in pairs, the pairs in couples and know
that we were cared for as we slept. Lined
and puffy-eyed in our robes we sit around
the breakfast table yawning, while he goes

out to stretch before his morning run.
Oh to be the insomniac, whose morning light
is Sirius, who has no promises to keep.
We envy him the way we envy anyone
who doesn't have children to listen for at night,
who doesn't check them twice before he sleeps.

ᗐᕽ Biology

For three months I injected mice
with powdered thyroid hormone. I was nice
to them at first, as skilled a murderess
as any in the end. I learned to hold
their bodies arched across
my knuckles, tails clenched
tightly in my pinky and the skin
behind their bristled ears pinched
between thumb and forefinger,
forcing them to bare their pin-
point fangs and giving me
a straight shot to the stomach.

The earliest deaths were accidental:
a Yellow slumped beneath the water
bottle, another pressed
behind a drawer. I killed
two Reds with my own bare
hands by piercing the esophagus. Then
the Blues turned cannibal, and I slammed
one on the floor in panic.

Once the Science Fair was over,
and my third place ribbon hung
limply on the wall, Ingie Svenson
said he wanted them
for pets. My mother told me
it was wrong to take advantage
of his courtship, that this boy
would get the worst of me
by taking those mice home.
But I pocketed his money, learned
to dodge his calls—so quick
was I to disinherit them all.

Sometimes I hear his broken Swedish
falling through my dreams
like a sigh, and I think it may be
Ingie talking down some rodent
from its hyperthyroid high—
Ingie with his mixing bowl of hair,
the white mouse with its bright blue
band of dye, Ingie's thick
endearments making flight seem
useless, the reddened glassy eye
of the mouse rising like the sun
to meet his blue eyes, full
of love, my hand upon the syringe
like a gun.

↙ Breakfast in Key West

The tablecloths are membrane-pink
and the white light falling
through the gumbo-limbo sets them
vibrating with expectation.
Food comes on a plate in the shape
of a lagoon, with bright green petals
of kiwi floating in the pale
yellow foam of an egg. With my eyes
I embrace my friends and beyond them
all of Duval Street, the shops
with their tinsel-framed doors,
houses tiered like birthday cakes,
the garland of palms that rings
the island and mile after mile
of shallow green sea where coral
gathers itself in baskets
and fish scatter in the wind.

My arms rise involuntarily
in a gesture not quite
of ownership but of one who expects
to receive everything: the motions
of sleep on a houseboat with walls
that wink and shimmer, where the air
chimes with every breath, swelling
and subsiding in a music
that is never the same; friendships
that probe and descend like the mangrove,
their tangled arches a landfall
for the ready survivor.

Late at night, in the still pools
of conversation, we feel the allegiances

rocking slowly, shifting beneath us.
There is talk almost constantly
of not going back, of finding
some minimal trade to ply and joining
the loose pastel throngs that swarm
the pier at sunset. The tightrope artist
in Mallory Square jokes about the woman
he left behind in Oneonta, making us believe
that we, too, can face death
from six feet up and laugh
at where we have lived for love.

One by one I shed my associations:
the sand at dawn is cool and blond
as sand. The palms have no branches
for cutting and stacking against
the wind, which fills my skirt
with a rustle of legs. I am tawny
and contented as the strays who litter
the streets, indifferent to all meals
but this one: its pale
pink tables like clouds,
its faces forever within my reach.

PART III

The
Whole
of
Longing

✌ Today a Wedding

We sleep too long, eat our oatmeal too fast.
You're late for work and rush off promising
to return early. I pack our warmest socks
for the honeymoon; it will be cold
in Amsterdam this time of year.

Already the sky is dark. Our clothes stand
flat against the bed: your gray suit,
our white shirts, my gray dress.
The sleeves touch in innocence.

But somewhere your tie and my scarf
lie tangled in a drawer, and at a predictable hour
my mother will cry herself to sleep,
secretly pleased for a daughter gone bad

on foreign soil whose marriage, like hers
is sudden, solitary, and choked with love.
She will finger my sister's wedding dress
(still vacuum-sealed) and recall that her dress was gray.

Like a piece of advice one might have followed
years ago, my girlish dreams seem small
and impractical against this ominous November
sky. But today, a wedding:
no guns, no bells.

✒ Nude at the Ironing Board

Here the body's longings are pressed
into service as guardians of the rolled
hem, the felled seam. Here
it is possible to see all longing
as flat, endless, its features
rippled or creased but never raised,
never for long. There is a rhythm
here that holds back as much
as it gives, and steam that rises,
spent, from the exhausted folds.
My mother ironed sheets, as if
to smooth the unevenness of desire
from her thoughts; would often press
thirty or forty shirts at a sitting.
They'd hang like tired children
from the doorknobs, waiting to be sent
to their rooms. If you were to paint me
here you would hang my clothes
from the door, use the muslin sky
pressed to the window for backlight, call
the steam "mist" and let it rise
from my ankles, lift the hem of hair
from my face where it hangs like a curtain,
holding back the light.

✒ The Snow, Among Other Things

This snow brings down a season
of forgetting, of laying desire down
like frozen limbs in the silence
of a drift. A season, too, of concentration
on minor motions—the table at breakfast,
the window at noon, the door
at dusk; not waiting but learning
not to wait, not to open
the door and see whose head
is moving in snowy silence along the wall.

This is winter's forgotten river;
see where the boats have left their lines
in the ice. The currents are still.
They have forgotten what they were running
from. Ice grows from the arms inward,
obscuring the tides and parting forever
land from water, the silent
from the still. We cannot see
the bottom but must think
the mud still groans there
when it cannot slide to sea.

This sky knows its place; it falls
at a time that is right for forgetting, obscuring
distant scenes, reducing landscape
to weight on white. Winter's first snow
drops softly, like a shawl drops
from a woman's shoulders in a moment
of distraction, reaching for a book
or an embrace.

✍ Mean Time, Greenwich

Two plums propped in a dusty bowl:
This is the place where East meets West,
this dusky crease, smelling faintly of earth
and paper bag. It is difficult to say at this
time (which the world's chronometer tells us
is right) who's leaning on whom.

The old Observatory rules the scene
like an ancient curfew: Children play
in silence at its feet. A genteel gray
pervades the room, and one by one
my plans for the afternoon
are extinguished. It is the eve
of our unfaithfulness.

In the West, you assume your work with some
importance; the columns rise gracefully at your feet.
Why do I see such violence in my third cup
of tea, bang my watch in vain against
the table? The shadowed East bears down.
The plums are no longer round.

Tonight, the hemispheres will nudge each other
softly, cling perhaps, ripen slowly, while
the Great Meridian steals down the slippery
hillside, divides a house, cuts off
a people from their past, strikes
a dozing publican between the eyes.

✺ The Compliment

He came on like a week
in the Bahamas: hot, predictable
and not to be trusted. He said
he'd photographed the fighting in Iran
and snapped my face in all
its postures of defense. He leaned
across the table to pay
for drinks, safari shirt
unsullied by the evening's powerful
humidity. Then he winked
and told me I looked tasty
in that sweater. His stylized
advances were amusing, and god knows
I wanted the attention, his eyes
on my cleavage like a bunker
in a desert war. He said
he wanted me for one
half hour against a wall,
no strings, and like the sea
my body swelled, my clothes
receded. Then friends appeared,
and to this day I wince
when I'm reminded of that precipice
of longing. But then he called
me "tasty"—a compliment
I've savored ever since.

✺ The Newlyweds

That they are young, or blond
should not be held against
them. Nor should the fact
that they do not resemble
us at any age. Let's admire
the colors she wears, the swaying
greens and oceanic blues, the way
his glasses stand at the bridge
of his nose, shaping our vision.
Hear them in the upstairs shower,
singing softly to each other.
Their harmonies sift through
the floors like dust and will
not be disturbed. I stand here,

an old scar thickening
in the sunlight, thinking
of the turbulence contained
by every weather, even this
settled afternoon. What can
they know of betrayal
in the kitchen, of the fierce
love for a sick child
and the regret that always,
always pillows our heads
in sleep? They are twins,
their golden heads inclined
as they eat beneath the chandelier.
Their mouths hold a language
we will not try to remember

tonight, as we sit before
the fire warming our fears,

a telephone on the table
between us. They don't
need me to tell them
how safe they are.

ꜱ꜠ *Flying Over Connecticut*

I appreciate the risks, perched
over this winter landscape
like a woman with her period over
a white brocade chair, expecting
any moment the humiliation
of a fall. Below, the house
of a woman whose husband kissed
me once as she bent to serve
canapés in an adjoining room,
a kiss so shadowy and swift
it might have been the passing
of a plane. From this altitude

there are no wrongs, only
the square white fields
of longing, roadways pulsing
with cars, each containing
a woman intent upon
her destination, driving toward
or away from happiness. Perhaps
I needed something by which to mark
an undistinguished evening, or the start
of a life of recklessness. It was
as if the whole of longing
had been quick-frozen to a moment
in Connecticut, as much a landmark
as the sudden flash of sunlight
off a skating pond. He may be

the diamond on the back of that black
snake of a road, or dreaming
his way into a thicket of despair.
But I tell you now, for weeks

I held that kiss like the fixed
pattern of frost on a window, surprised
by its delicate two-dimensionality,
always looking through, beyond.

🖎 Photograph of a Storm at Watch Hill

They are all here: the faithful
photographer in his city clothes,
choosing the pointless red stubble
of beach fence to contain his view;
the neglected lover slouched behind
the sea wall, nursing his gold
tooth and finding the ocean's angry swells
unbearably voluptuous. Somewhere
the husband runs circles around the scene,
swinging a child like a pail of water.

In the gray distance, a lighthouse beams
its sullen warning: It is the storm
that sucks color from the sky, that disfigures
perspective, marring all sense
of the time left to us, drawing us
to its biting edge. It is not a question
of danger; a woman who brings
these three men with her
is not in danger. But if she leaves
them there they will fall
to bickering among themselves over who
gets what—her way with words,
Christmas with her family, the photographs
like this one framed by all
she knows, and would forget

⚜ Midsummer

A rich man on his back
in the sun owns
this day, the season
he holds in his curled
palm, warm
with every pale breast
that has lingered there
with the idle, pleasant weight
of small change. The sun
heaps perfection on skin
already the color of fine
furniture, its coverings cast
aside, and somewhere a wife
rearranges his features for dusting
by a girl whose hair
turns ginger in the kettle's
copper light.

What can he want, why
open his eyes even once
to see if a woman bends
near or a willow teases
his ear with its lacework
of shadow and air? He has
his work, cool
in its tumbler of glass and children
who already see the diamonds
in a shaft of light. He sleeps
the sleep of the well-to-do,
awash in the sun's hard cash.

✐ August

No seduction, clothes
slumped on the floor like kids
who've been told
to *Get lost.* We're
here because there isn't
another person or place
that would have us, the world
fed up with our summer
recombinations, old
lovers circling the bed
like smoke. A season
when we should all
stay home and watch
snails drag
through the ash in our gardens—
any small torture kinder
than this, these
kisses flung free
of your mouth like the hook
and you're gone, tail
weaving the shadows that ring
your eyes with a lake
of their own August brown.

◢ September

A season ends
on a yellow verandah scraped
by leaves, swept clean
by a light rain. A season
ends, here where it began
in a play of light across
your face, this time
so quick and sharp it comes
closer to the razored light
of winter, whose deprivations
I find I welcome. A season
ends because it has to,
because the summer light
is paradoxical, golden
with possibility and bent
almost to the ground by the weight
of its blossoming. I say
our lives are ruled
by such seasons and your eyes
flash blue with the brief
anger of autumn, then
fall. A season ends
with this acknowledgment of endings,
one man bowing to his own
loss, cigarette sifting
through air while behind him
the sun turns coalish,
determined to keep
what is barely day alive.

✺ Indian Summer

The unseasonable warmth, unnatural
darkness of late afternoon on this

the first day of our return
to Eastern Standard Time

remind me of a man I met at a dinner party
who gazed at his wife—sinking

into the sofa like an August sun, all
pinks and golds, the last flash

of emerald from her throat as she glanced
our way—and said to me,

Isn't she perfect? No one knows
what to say about this weather,

or about a man who loves his wife
so much he tells a stranger,

or so little he buys her an emerald
to assuage whatever. But if this

is what precedes winter, let's
give it a name, savage

and serene, and call love
marriage out of season.

◝ Excuses

Saturday night, November. We're
calculating what we've spent
anticipating winter: two
storm doors, a kerosene heater,
three cords of wood, five
long coils of putty to stuff
in the cracks once swollen
with summer's urgent breath.
The room is cold, but we'll hold
off burning one more night.

The phone rings. A friend announces
another marital collapse. The news
shocks us in a way we cannot
name, the way it shocks
us when the leaves collapse
in color and just let go,
although it is familiar,
and we cannot name
their lingering precipitation.

We return to our accounting, less
appalled by our own extravagant
precautions. We're more than ready
to excuse them, to blame it
on his job, her lack of style.
We talk about their house (the one
we almost bought), recount
the parties we attended there
on warmer nights than this. I ask
you if you love me, leave
the room, return to find
your bolt gray eyes upon me
like the season: summer's cost.

PART IV

In
This
a Celebration

🌿 Underwater

I think what I think
is my last thought:
that for years I've lived
the untethered life
of a strong swimmer
only to find, here
in the urban blue
of the Pacific, I'm
a sinker like everyone else.

Waves tower and fold
above me like tall
buildings—street
after street of them.
Suddenly I am old,
mugged by the surf, trapped
in foam thicker than any smog,
killed off by August.
My chest swells
like a tree trunk. The string
of my bikini grows inward,
old barbed wire.

I'm losing my sense
of humor, can't remember
what irony is, except
to die on vacation.
So this is the calm
they spoke of, those women
with babies strapped
to their chests, their backs,
whose eyes said *I'm drowning.*
And this, the man they reached for
in the water of their laundry tubs:

rising before me like pandanus,
tight-skinned and many-rooted
saying hold my arm, take
a breath, hold tight.

A rogue emerges
from the jungle of the waves.
The dark shape surges
but its tonnage barely sways
the grasses of his arm as it lifts us
toward shore. I suck
air, kiss the sharp rocks
repeatedly with my knees,
vomit salt water, lift my head and see
for the first and last time
a hero, the underwater kind.

 Postpartum

(for Amy)

Already you would kill
for sleep—your husband,
for the soft click-click
of membranes in the dark
slumberous passages; the cats,
for their narrow stretch of sunlight
on the dusty floor. Small
blankets spasm and billow
like the earth along a fault.
Their satin rustlings
swallow night whole.

Less than a month has passed
since you tore the pockets
from your husband's shirt,
thinking surely this
is the worst. Pain
is a witch that way,
motherhood her spell. Now
you know it is the weight
of your own arms
on a winter night
nursing in the dark.

No one knows
about the time your head
snapped to consciousness:
how long had the radio
been hissing like that?
The cars outside
made a continuous rushing

sound, like water.
With every limb
you listened, taut
with fear. Nothing.
Then slowly returned
to a dream of sleep
in which you slept
a daughter's deep,
unruffled sleep.

I could tell you
about the day you will wear
motherhood like an old
cardigan, worn to lightness
and pulled tight against
the chill. But what you need
is a miracle—not like birth
but like the baby who grows fat
on your thin blue milk.

The Swimming Lesson

I.

I make a game of it: Ring
around the Rosy. Gripping
her small slippery sides I dance,
moon-like, through the water.
Her lungs suck in terror
like air. At two and a half
she knows what it means to go under,
fingers clawing in disbelief.
My arm goes up her back like a tree,
my fingers branch in the trembling
of her hair.

II.

I am twelve again, about
to be baptized. The only thing
I believe in is death by water.
I take a deep breath, cross
my hands against the bones of my chest
and surrender what little faith
I might have had. Submerged,
I open my eyes and see the tall
green boots of a fisherman. Wet
robes billow and cling like clouds.
I did not know heaven would smell
like a Toni in the kitchen sink.
I crumple at the waist, begin
to flail.

III.

This is my only child. She is old
enough to understand a betrayal.
The water fans to stillness
around us. Her eyes still
say *That time you let
me go.* Ashes, ashes.

✎ Conversation in Key West

She seized a lime by the skull
and reamed the pulp
from the rind. *To break
it down,* she explained.
*It's the only way to make
a Margarita.* Back from Spain
in her Alpenstocks and cropped
gray hair, she looked like a woman
of sixty grown into a boy
of twenty-two. She spoke
of her translations, how
she'd become the Spanish poet's
confidante. *Next I'll go
to Grenada. He has family there.*

A Phantom from the base nearby
screamed low across the sky.
*That's where death comes
from. I lost my husband
at twenty-nine in a naval plane
that was never found, and eight
years later my son, electrocuted
when he fell from a tree he'd climbed
against my will, near the home
of a man I no longer loved, in a state
I had not wanted him to visit.*

One thing I've learned, she said:
You attract what you fear most.
Already I could feel the poem
rising like a vapor trail
behind me, sinking
under the knowledge
that it could not be unwritten.

53

✺ Hypothermia

How he skated through the livingroom
without so much as raising a cat's
cocked ear is the first miracle. The second,
how he stepped off the porch
into a drift so astonishingly soft
and deep he surrendered to the dream and fell
asleep upon the quilted yard. He must
have seen the snow glittering like mica
in the granite sky and been too young
to understand it could not be
extracted. Or wondered if his parents
would reward him when he spilled
his fist of diamonds in their startled laps.

The cop who saved him said
his limbs were "filled with slush"
when they brought him in. I read
all this aloud at dinner,
in that emphatic tone reserved for mute
comparisons. My husband finds me
morbid, inclines his look
as if to say he has no sleeping
fears. While silent at the sink
in perfect concentration, our only
child palpates a cylinder of lemonade
in its softened cardboard sleeve.

~~ The Swing

I could see the child flailing
in the dirt-filled hollow below
the swing, comical almost in her rolled
pink tights and puffy lavender
coat, her Sunday shoes
too scarred for shining. From the jungle
gym's shadow her mother limped
toward her, arranged their shapes
awkwardly for comfort. When she spoke
I saw her mouth was off-center,
the white balloon in a Sunday comic
awaiting its caption: "Is she
all right? Is she all right?"

This question from one eye
and then the other, seamed
at the corners and searching
my face from two directions. Her stubby
fingers pawed at the little girl's
satiny bangs while I examined her
for signs of injury. Undisturbed,
the child reached for her mother's chin,
which bristled with sturdy and stumped
black hairs: a carnival face,
a face seen from the sealed windows
of the station wagon on a Sunday drive
through Newark, my father warning us
not to look too hard, too long.

*   *   *   *

Tonight at the table, shuddering with cut
glass and colored sauces, our Chinese hostess

speaks haltingly of her childhood escape,
how they starved her father and cut
his sun-taut body in pieces
to teach the villagers a lesson.
Her husband clears the table and carries
their son down the silk-papered hall
to bed. I tell my story of birth's
accidents, how some are taken
from their mothers in the night
while others fly through the sunlight
on swings, fall, and are not afraid.

🍂 *Love Letters*

Three bundles, neatly bound with threadbare
ribbon and girlish care, stacked on the hearth
like expensive kindling: limbs of the past,

pruned this morning from a closet's dense
debris and set aside for burning in the stove's
black heart. With a daughter in school

who soon will read as easily as she idles
here, freeing their unstuck stamps,
no written history is secure.

Who chose this day—the sky immune,
the windows blank with cold—to loose
their lovebound heat? She wants to know

why I feed them singly to the flames,
pausing every third or fourth to lift
a compliment from their skin-like folds.

How can I tell her there were others,
that lives were leased before her birth?
She sees in this a celebration: her mother's

face intensely lit, lips fingering
another childhood story. She sits in my lap,
folding airplanes, when the light begins

to change. Together we relinquish play
to comfort, words to fire, chant
their names: Good-bye Michael, Carl, James.

🌿 Girl of Four

I won't buy her a gun, so she makes
one with her hand, its nails deliberate
as bullets, grimy as steel. She picks
the girls off one by one, calling them
by the faults they will die for: crybaby,
tattletale, scaredy-cat. They turn
their ruffled backs to the wind and gather
their skirts in a circle, falling

in and out of each other's graces
as easily as if in a dance. She arrives
at school dressed for battle in her birthday
fatigues, so skilled at camouflage
she could be one of them, her body
as stripling-thin, the skin of her cheeks
as apple-innocent as theirs. A boy of five
springs from his mother's car, rams her

from the side. She rolls in a tuck
through the garden mulch and is back
on her feet, eyes poised for a parry.
I picture her at dawn, standing by
our bed in her nightie, pausing to release
the breath that pulls me from my sleep,
then slipping in between us. Already
she knows that a woman cannot wait

to arm herself, that she must know
how to shoot and how to draw a smile
from the rifle's angry eye. She holds a rubber
nipple between her legs and calls
for me, stands there on the blood red
stairs above my head, grinning
bayonets, saying I can be all
those things you told me and more.

A Father to His Daughter

In my day, it was the custom
when two prep-school glee clubs
met to guarantee each quavering
boy a date by tethering him
to someone his own height.
The clubs would sit beside
each other in the auditorium,
and as their names were called out
mount the stage in twos to greet
the evening's fate. They called
me first, and as I stood
there like a tremolo
they called her name,
and from her seat she rose
and rose an octave or more
above me. Then, to the descant
of my fellow singers' hoots began
her slow glissando to the stage.
I remember that her belt
was pink and gold, that her torso
was encased in pale pink oxford
cloth and that it stretched out
like a whole note that could be
sustained beyond the evening's end.
Her hair was pale and pleated
like her skirt, which ran
up and down the register for miles.
My eyes, awkward at her buttons,
sought hers and saw there
such forgiveness for my size,
my broken tenor, the sort of evening
we would spend together,
with the colored lights so tangled

in her hair it didn't seem
to matter if my fortunes rose
or settled in the perfumed air
between us.

        I know this seems
to you a crude device for bringing
girls and boys together. But when
you're at the dance tonight, remember
that women are superior at heart
because they've studied singing,
because they know
that harmony is a gift both
from above and from below.

✍ *A Mother to Her Daughter*

There was a man, I never told
your father. Having said this
I can see Oxford, June-green
and glistening with bells, his broad
black-robed shoulders moving
against the golden stones
of the University.

Remember the month we spent
in the Cotswolds, starved for sun
and sick to death of the Ashmolean?
We were off to lunch at The Bear
(The Boar? The Trout?) when I stopped
to ask on the Banbury Road a gray-
haired woman in blue-gray tweed
if she knew of the place. She leaned
on the gate as the car pulled away
and frowned at her bulbs, their hair
in the dirt, their legs
in the cold spring air.

That was his house, and behind
its shuttered stare his study, deep
in shadow, in books and photographs
of his children, those spherical
cheeks and haircuts like thick
clay bowls. On a plane to Boston
once I watched the spires flatten
to specks beneath me.

I tell you this now
so that when you hear the gray
whispering at your temples, see

the roads of Oxfordshire unwind
across your face, you will know
what you have forsaken
and for what.

༄ Biceps

are what separate us, her mother
said. In my day women
gave their bodies away, watched
their chests contract with milk
then sink back into the apostrophe
of dress. Now it seems imperative
that childless women raise
five-pound weights to maturity.
Not that I think it's wrong
to sit there in that second
purple skin of yours and make
those slow parentheses in air.
But why? Already you could press
that skinny boyfriend to a comma.
I've read that women who reduce
their body fat below a certain
point stop having periods.

Enough. Let me lift you
from the floor and see if I
can tell the difference between a child
and the dead weight of wet laundry.
If my back holds, you can tell
your friends that fitness
is hereditary: I've worked
my muscles sore in raising you.

PART V

This Body of Silk

✍ Birthdays

The radio intones the day, the hour
and hisses out the New York
weather: hazy, hot and humid,
showers almost impossible. Tearing
myself from the flesh of my dreams I send
my legs to the floor and notice
my knees are frowning—not the first
time my body has spoken for me.

My mother telephones on the hour
of my birth. I was the easiest of her five
deliveries. She describes the dark-haired
infant, streaked with gentian violet,
and how she cried for the pink
bundle of her imaginings.

I jog twice the usual distance,
down a road whose broken face
leads me to where and what
I have been: chased by a boy
in grade school once, legs
thrashing under crinolines; the morning
of my wedding, heels hammering
down the marble hall.

In the haze cast by my pounding, a hot
air balloon moves silently
up the river. What are birthdays
but the impulse to charge each shadow
with a humid significance, brought on
by age and the lengthening light? Take
this body of silk, rising gracefully
on a puff off the river, sinking
to meet the not yet visible earth.

ᘓ Knees

Now I'll never be
what I never was as a girl,
what a friend called me
once from her car window,
wind lifting her frosted
curls, the wattle of flesh
waving at me from her underarm
as I pumped my calves
up the hill. *You look
so athletic,* she said
and all the years of awkward
slow motion, the blundering
on dates, the dances ruined
by hemispheres of sweat
fell away like a road
tilting suddenly downward.
I ran like a cameraman, backwards,
facing myself and seeing
my legs the way an architect
might see them—tendons working
invisibly, the cables from which
even age could be suspended.

Now my knees complain
every time I trust them
with my weight. I want
to punish my body for leaving me
so unsatisfied, for teaching
me what those rope-muscled
boys in high school knew
all along: that all running
is running away, the body's
escape from longing, the longing

to escape desire that sweeps
down from the sky like a swallow
chasing a moving train,
distracting the engineer,
or the bee that swims a spiral
around the marathoner's head.

My knees grind with the cumulative
pain of love that goes
untended for years. They creak
like the stairs I mount
for sleep. I hear them
shifting in the night like burglars
on the ground floor, filling
their sacs with the slow
theft of cartilage. In dreams
I fall into your arms, bones
giving in to time
and time again.

When You Go to the Funeral

fix your eyes
on a green wallpaper rose.
Watch it swell
and fade.
Would you wear
a dress with roses
to your grave?

Wonder if he slept
with every woman
in the room. Suspect
the ones who gather,
still and glassy-eyed
on the meniscus
of tears.

Did you break
and enter only to find
the earring you hoped
to leave behind?
And was the robe
flung open on the bed
an enticement
or a warning
that even young men
can be spent
by morning?

Think about his withered
leg, how you knew
about it before you
knew him; knew,
too, his mother was dead

before he knew it, saw
the note and said
nothing.

Ignore the eulogist
who mourns
the untimely death
of a fine
administrator. Think
about his hands
what they did
to your pink sweater.

ᔰ The Sinking of the Marques

(for Susan Howell, Navigator)

The watch had just ended. Everyone
else asleep down below. A sudden
squall swallowed the stars, rolled
the ship over in her sleep.
There was no time for knowing,
the first survivor tells us. Now
another returns, ghost-eyed, says
a warning rang, there were screams
from the companionway. A struggle for life
jackets, small sacrifices that mean
nothing now. The ship inhaled,
heeled over and sailed to the bottom.

Each truth brings us closer
to drowning. We sleep lightly, one eye
on the stars, ears tuned to the fine
pitch of darkness. I think of the woman
I knew only slightly until now:
how she taught the crew dead
reckoning, the meals she cooked
and froze for her family
before leaving, how she said
in her postcard this
was the time of her life.

We have our consolations:
There is a slow grandeur in the words
when a tall ship goes down;
her children can always say,
She was lost at sea. Her friends
lay a wreath on the ocean's lip.
Later we find it locked

in debris, the foliage slack,
blossoms swollen in their sockets.

When I was young I worked
as a lifeguard: preened all summer
in my high white chair. But tonight
I dream in the lap of the swimmer, still
on my back in the deep end's
deep blue waste. Above me
the fat boy paces his double
back flips. I see him coming
toward me like an eclipse.

✺ Letter to Diane

This August afternoon
of vivid lawn and swooping sky
I spend painting white
fence whiter than it has a right
to be. Each brush stroke
adds an hour to its wooden
life, each coat perhaps a year.
Somewhere in Maryland, they've strapped
you down for radiation, drawn a square
upon your chest, a great
hulk of machinery your sun
and now you're sweating with despair.
We've talked about this since
I can remember, where
it might recur, whether
you should go ahead and have
a child as if your life depended
on that ordinary show of faith.
When they cut your breast
off, it was still a loss to shape
your life around. Now

all this talk of bones—
bone tired, skin and bones—
takes absence as its art.
When they said your sternum
was a shell, I saw a bone-white
cockle where your heart
should be. If I thought
leaving this page blank
would turn the cancer back,
I'd make this line
my last. But words can only
satisfy the hours, not consume.

74

Diane, sometimes I'm blinded
by the whiteness here. My bikini fills
with sweat that will not fall,
even as I curl and straighten, bend
and scrape to remedy this wall
where mold has eaten through and will
again, some day when this
white yields to mottled gray, and green
moves on from emerald to verdigris,
as seen through more forgiving eyes.

﹏ The Death of Uncles

There are four of us in the car. We are fifth
in a line of six cars, fewer than a man
should have to show for his seventy years.
The weather is barely visible, but we all
strain to see it. We pass the pond
where, years ago, my father took us
every Sunday while my mother went up
the hill to watch her father stare
at the window beyond which we played,
sullenly, by the crusted edge of a pond.

Who can prepare us for the death of uncles
we barely knew? Who can spare us the details
of their suffering before breakfast, when the phone
sends sleep scattering like a broken flock
of birds and we stiffen against the intruder? Who
is there to tell us when we lift our children
from sleep like fresh laundry from a deep drawer
and bury our faces in the folds of their throats that each
of our pleasures is numbered, and those we do not
name fall from our arms with the least commotion?

The widow's coat is shaking in the wind. We pay
our respects obediently, like children avoiding a kiss.
Remember now the uncle who photographed weddings,
birthdays, anniversaries with the heads cut off,
the vital partner missing, a dismembered but adoring
hand draped across the unknowing shoulder
of the celebrant, the children in the background somewhere
running, shaking their hair in the wind.

✍ Unk at Eighty-four

I didn't go to the funeral—instead
I spent my morning here in bed,
bent and curled like a fiddlehead

in longjohns, dreaming of the ball we played
behind the school, the way I slid
into third, leaning like a shadow on the wall.
And how the sun stayed
in the sky forever when we were kids.
Lord I miss my brother Paul.

My pleasures are remembered now:
lunch at Dempsey's with my friends
the day the Champ walks in;
living long enough to grind a lens,

to feel the oiled endlessness of time
beneath my palm. I'd like to take
my stamps to London, visit every dealer
on the Strand. If I could just climb
the steps to the post office, or make
a sandwich. They call time the healer

but he's wounded me too often.
I see my baby sister's face
criss-crossed by grief at sixty-one.
Her death's the only fear left
to me, now she's lost that ribbon waist
and tells me she takes calcium.

Did I shave? I can't remember
when, or why I never took a wife.
Now Paul is gone and it's November: the lawn
won't need mowing again in this life.

✒ An Old Man Falls

How unlike a tower of blocks, or building
toppled by the wind, where first there is a nodding
as if in expectation or assent, the way an old man
lets his head roll one way and his eyes
another just before he falls asleep. This
fall started below his feet, and I could only
think of earthquakes, with the table stretched out
like a continent between us. They say the cows in Santa
Rosa knew that San Francisco would be sprawling
in the dust, but they could only mill about the yard
and swing their heads. I, too, anticipate the slide
of plates and glasses as he leaves the table, know
what objects will be lost forever in the fault.

An old man falls so slowly—perhaps
he wants to make it last, his feet slipping
away from their shadowed soles, ankles rolling to one side,
the frightened parallel of shins leaning into the sloping
floor like a skier about to lose his edge.
Nor will he let me help
him up, but sits there planning how
he will rebuild himself: climbing on all fours
to first a stool, then hoisting his collapse
of hips onto a chair, and finally taking life
by the door jambs. How like a child learning
to walk, who knows that somewhere down the hall
or on a day as still as this one, the legislators
of the house will bring him down again.

Or like those grand hotels in every fading
city, whose rooms have housed the greats in their prime,
then fall into disrepair, are briefly used to shelter
the needy, and then one day they're detonated
by an expert crew and simply lose their footing,
falling more like a man than a ton of bricks.

A NOTE ON THE AUTHOR

Sue Ellen Thompson is a graduate of Middlebury College, and she received her M.A. from the Bread Loaf School of English. Her poems have appeared in *Tendril, New Letters, Denver Quarterly, Poet Lore,* and other magazines. She was the 1982 National Arts Club Scholar at the Bread Loaf Writers' Conference and won first prize in the Connecticut Writers' League's 1984 National Writing Awards. As one of ten poets selected to participate in CONNTOURS, a touring performing artists' program sponsored by the Connecticut Commission on the Arts, she has given readings throughout the state as well as the rest of New England and New York. She lives in Mystic, Connecticut, where she is a freelance writer and an associate editor for *Tendril* magazine.

A NOTE ON THE PRIZE

The Samuel French Morse Poetry Prize was established in 1983 by the Northeastern University Department of English in order to honor Professor Morse's distinguished career as teacher, scholar, and poet. The members of the prize committee are Francis C. Blessington, Joseph deRoche, Susan Goldwitz, Victor Howes, Stuart Peterfreund, and Guy Rotella.